T0353859

NAMES TRULY HAVE MEANING
AND
POWER

Whose Name Are You Representing?

Print information available on the last page.

Rev. date: 12/14/2018

To order additional copies of this book, contact:
Xlibris
1-888-795-4274
www.Xlibris.com
Orders@Xlibris.com

JAHMELLO L. ISHMAEL ZUÑIGA

GENESIS

1-9:11

WITH
URGENCY AND CLARITY
Vol. 1

INSPIRING NEW BOOK

GENESIS
WITH URGENCY AND CLARITY

VOL.1

By
JAHMELLO L. ISHMAEL ZUÑIGA

WRITTEN TO INFORM AND REMIND ALL HUMAN BEINGS ABOUT:

1. **GOD'S CHARACTER**
2. OUR CHARACTER
3. THE DIRECTION THAT THE WORLD IS HEADING
4. WHY **GOD'S FINAL JUDGEMENT** MUST COME
5. HOW OUR INDIVIDUAL CHOICE WILL EFFECT US
6. WHO WILL BE **SAVED** IN THAT GREAT DAY OF JUDGEMENT
7. THE **GREAT REWARD GOD** HAS FOR US

THE HOLY BIBLE—GOD'S SPOKEN WORD—WAS NOT GIVEN TO CONFUSE US; BUT TO PREPARE US!!!

JAH LOVE

Dedications

6-19-03

WITH LOVE AND HOPE, I DEDICATE THIS EXTREMELY IMPORTANT VOL. 1 BOOK TO MY SONS, DAUGHTERS, NIECES, NEPHEWS, COUSINS, IN-LAWS CHILDREN, FRIENDS CHILDREN, AND THE CHILDREN OF THE WORLD. BECAUSE THE FULFILLMENT OF GOD'S WORD IS NEAR, DO NOT ALLOW YOURSELVES TO GET BLINDED BY THE IRRESPONSIBLE ACTS OF THOSE WHO WORK HARD NOT TO UNDERSTAND THIS NOTICE. FOR MANY, THIS DAYS AND THE DAYS TO COME, ARE UNCERTAIN ONES. BUT TO YOU WHO SEEK THE TRUE MESSAGE OF GOD'S WORD, TO YOU WILL BE GIVEN THE TRUE UNDERSTANDING OF THE SAVIOR'S CERTAINTY FOR THE WORLD. ALL THAT IS ASKED OF YOU BY THE ALMIGHTY, IS TO <u>TRUST IN THE EVERLASTING PROMISE</u> AND TO <u>LIVE ACCORDINGLY.</u>

INTRODUCTORY STATEMENT

IN STAGES OF GREAT <u>POWER</u>, <u>DIRECTION</u>, AND <u>CONSIDERATION</u>, **GOD** MADE ALL THE EXCEPTIONAL THINGS THAT MANY PEOPLE OF THE PAST AND PRESENT CONTINUE TO QUESTION, BECAUSE OF THEIR INTENSE <u>CURIOSITY</u> AND <u>DISBELIEF</u>. AS A RESULT OF THESE TWO <u>UNCHANNELED</u> DEFECTS, MANY HAVE <u>ALLOWED</u> THEMSELVES TO BE LEAD ASTRAY, FROM THE ACTUAL TRUTH ABOUT OUR EXISTENCE AND THE **REALITY** OF THE **ALMIGHTY.**

For a very long time, branches of science have been giving their <u>intellectual opinions</u> about the formation of these and other heavenly bodies.

11-11-02

In the beginning **GOD—ONE WHO IS TRULY GOOD, THE CREATOR, THE MORAL GOVERNOR, ONE WHO IS COMPASSIONATE, THE MERCIFUL, THE EVERLASTING, THE AGREEMENT MAKER, THE PROMISE KEEPER ...**made the things that our senses connect with in one form or another: <u>The Earth</u> (the chosen planet for life because of its given ability to produce and sustain the living), <u>Day and Night</u> (to allow the activities of life to occur), <u>Bodies of Water</u> (for drinking, washing, and irrigating the lands as well as providing a home to the various animals in it) <u>The Enormous Sky</u> (which serves as a covering for the earth's creations), <u>The Clouds</u> (for the production of rain), <u>The Great Lands</u> (to support our gravitational pull), <u>The Different Plants</u> (for health and growth), <u>The Sun</u> (for production of heat, light, rise and fall of the ocean) <u>The Moon</u> (for production of light as well as the rise and fall of the ocean) <u>The Rest of the Planets</u> (having their own special qualities and purposes), <u>The Stars</u> (serving as additional light for the earth during the night) and <u>All The Animals</u> that live on land. All these things GOD made in <u>Preparation of a Distinct</u> and <u>Set Apart Special Creation</u>. Once everything was in place GOD said, **"Let US—ALL THAT IS BENEFICIAL AND OF GREAT QUALITY AND WITHOUT OPPOSITION—form Human Beings to ACCOUNT for our REALITY. In addition to their existence, allow them to have the ABILITY to ACT in a greater capacity than all the animals of the earth."** As a result, GOD created the man and the woman in order for them to carry out <u>together</u> their special purpose of: 1.) providing the earth with a <u>new</u> supply 2.) becoming <u>many</u> in the world 3.) having <u>good</u> results in all things 4.) becoming <u>greater than all</u> that has been created on earth. GOD then told the man and the woman, **"Know that I have given YOU and ALL the animals of the earth, the various plants for production of health and growth."** After the completion of all that was made, GOD CONSIDERED EVERYTHING TO BE VERY APPROPRIATE.

The continent of Africa has produced the <u>oldest of human</u> fossils in the world.

This is how the first <u>HUMAN BEINGS, PLANTS</u> and <u>ANIMALS</u> came to exist in this distinct and special planet: **THE LORD GOD MOST POWERFUL OF ALL**—caused rain to fall, then formed the entire physical structure and substance of the first man from the excellent soil. In addition, the man received into his lungs the unique air of the earth to help him live. As a result, he possessed very distinctive qualities, such as: <u>THOUGHTS, FEELINGS</u>, and <u>THE ABILITY TO **MAKE DECISIONS.**</u> In addition, THE LORD GOD established a yard toward the east of **Eden** (<u>the agreeable place</u>) where human beings would live. In this yard, GOD made all the different plants to grow including those that in <u>our judgment</u> are good for health and growth. Among the plants that grew as a result of the strength that GOD gave the seeds were: THE TREE CONTAINING **LIFE** (<u>for continuous and prosperous living</u>) and THE TREE CONTAINING **KNOWLEDGE ABOUT GOOD AND BAD** (<u>knowledge that would be gained through DIFFICULT experiences because of DISOBEDIENCE</u>).

As for this place of occupancy, it had a river that served the yard to great extent because it irrigated the land to its fullest. As the flow of water went through the yard, <u>growth</u> and <u>beauty</u> to the many different plants became more and more apparent. Once the stream of water passed through the garden, it would separate itself into four great river resources: the first **Pison** (constant current), the second **Gihon** (constant current), the third **Hiddekel** (constant current), and the fourth **Euphrates** (constant current).

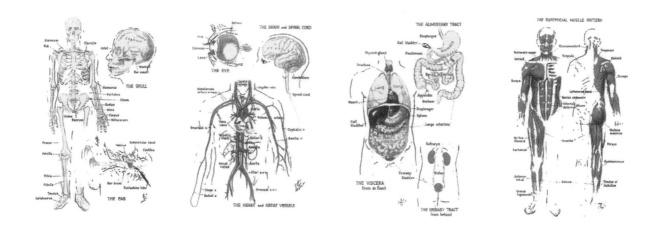

Our body parts are so unique, that duplicating them through scientific procedures can be very difficult; not to mention, <u>very dangerous!</u>

As for the man that was formed, GOD put him in the garden to <u>prepare</u> it and to <u>maintain</u> it. But God gave the man called **Adam**—<u>ONE WHO WAS FORMED FROM THE EXCELLENT SOIL OF THE EARTH</u>, <u>specific information</u> about the two special trees: Adam was first told, that he could STAY ALIVE and be <u>completely healthy forever,</u> by eating from the MANY plants specified. The second thing that was told to Adam, was that he should NOT eat from the SINGLE plant of the garden that would CANCEL the first fact. <u>Once GOD settled the future course of action</u> with Adam, GOD said, **"It is NOT proper that man should be by himself; I will make helpers of each kind to join him."** For this reason, GOD shaped every animal from the <u>same</u> soil that man was formed. After the animals were made, they were taken to Adam to be named at his DISCRETION. By having this authority, not only did Adam give the land animals their names but also described them by their genders. But from the different kinds of things that were created, there wasn't one that <u>resembled</u> Adam's **SPECIAL** characteristics <u>to join</u> him with the specific purpose of the designated land.

Although, affection is a clear characteristic that is found in many species of the world, <u>many scientists consider</u> some primates of the ape families to have had one common ancestor with that of human beings. <u>Their reasoning</u> is because of some shared attributes. Yet, <u>they can't explain why human beings</u> are so much more mentally advanced.

11-29-02

As a result, THE LORD GOD caused Adam's body and mind to become motionless in order to bring about another SPECIAL creation. So after Adam became inactive, THE LORD took one rib from his body and used it to shape the first **Woman.** Once this procedure was completed, GOD introduced the woman to Adam: Adam having full knowledge of how she came about said, "She is NOW bone of my bones and body of my body. She shall be called woman, because she was taken out of man. For this reason, shall a man LEAVE the source of his existence (referring to his parents) and give his LOYALTY to his mate. Now man alongside of his **EQUAL**, shall be ONE body." As for the man and the woman's appearance in the LORD'S chosen place, they were completely naked and at EASE. But from the rest of the four-footed animals that were put in the garden, the SERPENT DID NOT ACCEPT THE GREAT VALUE THAT GOD HAD PROCLAIMED TOWARDS HUMAN BEINGS. As a result, it asked the woman (not because she was an inferior creation, but because she happened to be close by at that time),"Is it true that GOD said, that you should not nourish yourselves with all the plants of the garden?" The woman then answered, "GOD said that we could eat from the production of the land, EXCEPT from the product of the plant that is in the middle of the garden. In addition, GOD instructed us NOT to touch it because our lives as we know it, would be ANNULLED." The serpent then responded by saying, "Your lives in fact shall not be put to an end, because GOD knows that in the time you eat from the plant, your mind shall be exposed to new experiences and you shall be equally respected because of what you will know." The woman after being PERSUADED to believe that the plant that GOD warned them about contained continuous health, growth, understanding, and higher status, ate from its production and gave some to her mate.

Because <u>many people will continue</u> to give themselves to ungodly pleasures, <u>one must seriously start thinking</u> about how one can be <u>set apart</u> from this present and future behavior.

As a result, both began to feel ASHAMED about their appearance and their DECISION of having gone against <u>GOD'S favorable instructions.</u> While being in the state of shame, they decided to put fig leaves together in order to cover their distinct body parts. At the time that they heard the voice of THE LORD GOD approaching them, during the calm day of their <u>Deliberate Disobedience</u>, they hid themselves among the plants of the garden. But when THE LORD GOD said to Adam, **"Where are you?"** (REFERRING TO THEIR PRESENT CONDITION) Adam's response was, "I heard your voice, but because of my appearance I became afraid, therefore I hid." GOD then asked, **"Who told you about your appearance? Have you eaten from the tree that I directed you NOT to eat from?"** (GOD is all knowing.   But GOD wants us to take <u>RESPONSIBILITY</u> for our ACTIONS). After being asked these DIRECT questions, <u>Adam became defensive</u> and said, "The woman that you introduced me to, gave me from the production of the tree." Once Adam gave his excuse, THE LORD GOD asked Adam's companion, **"What is this that you have done?"** The woman REMEMBERING the nature of GOD, gave no excuse and said, "The serpent <u>lead me to believe</u> something that was NOT so. Because of this, I ate from the tree."

As a result, <u>THE LORD GOD said to the serpent</u>, **"Since you have caused this, you are going to SUFFER more than all the four-footed animals of the land; with your body shall you get around. As a result, dust shall you take into your lungs for the rest of your existence. In addition to this, I will put a condition of UNFRIENDLINESS between you and the woman. This same condition will also exist between your descendants and her descendants. As a result, it shall cause HARM to your body as well as have an effect on your mental capacity. CONSEQUENTLY, you shall cause HARM to them that threaten your existence."**

The Serpent is the <u>ancestor</u> of modern snakes. Today, they vary in <u>size</u>, <u>color</u>, <u>strength</u>, and <u>habitat.</u> Snakes are also unusual animals, because by it being so close to the ground its entire body <u>senses all</u> motion around it.

<u>To the woman GOD said</u>, "**I will greatly increase your mental ANGUISH and the way in which you will bring children into the world. In PAIN shall you give birth. During this circumstance, your REQUEST for help shall be towards your companion. As a result, he shall impose authority over you.**" <u>To the man GOD said</u>, "**Because you CAREFULLY CONSIDERED AND IGNORED what was told to you about the tree, the land shall be in a state of great CONFUSION. As a result, with HARD WORK AND REGRET, shall you eat the plants from the land for the REMAINDER of your life. Because now, thorns and thistles shall it produce to you, until you return to the ground that you were made from.**" Because of all that had taken place, Adam named his partner, **Eve** (one who is RESPONSIBLE for what happend): Although Adam had SIMILAR <u>ideas</u> of being powerful, he considered Eve the cause of their present and future way of life. After the confirmation, regarding the future course of action that Adam and Eve were about to be faced with, THE LORD GOD made them clothes of animal fur for protection and said, "**Human Beings are now like one of US; to distinguish between RIGHT and WRONG.**" Now because of the danger that would have risen if they ate from the tree containing Life Everlasting, <u>THE LORD GOD sent Adam and Eve away</u> from the Garden of Eden and into the world they CHOSE for themselves (The Place Where They Would Begin Their Difficult Lives).

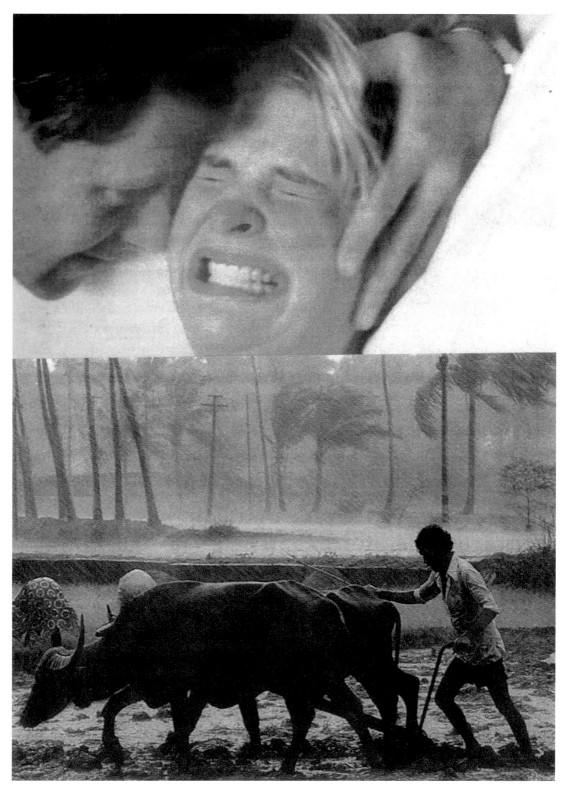

For many women, giving birth to a child <u>as well as having to deal with other life circumstances</u> continues to be very unbearable. As for the many men who are <u>attempting to escape the difficulties of this world</u>, know that your attempt will continue to be just that; <u>an attempt!</u>

12-25-02

As they left from the place of great Productivity, Beauty and Freedom, <u>GOD placed towards the east of it GUARDIANS and A BURNING SWORD</u> to illuminate in all directions for the purpose of protecting the location of the TREE having the great qualities of continuous and prosperous living. As a result of Adam and Eve's exile from GOD'S agreeable place for procreation and constant success, they had their first sexual experience outside of GOD'S plan, which then resulted in Eve's first difficult PREGNANCY. As time passed, Eve gave birth to a son named **Cain** (one who DOES NOT PRACTICE SELF-CONTROL). As a result of his birth, Eve said, "I have been given a male child from the Lord." Eve again, gave birth to another son named **Abel** (one who INDIRECTLY SUGGESTS): Abel became a <u>protector of sheeps,</u> while Cain became a <u>digger of the land</u>.

Now in the progress of time, Cain brought with him the production of the land which had no value and presented it to THE LORD. Abel also brought THE LORD a presentation (The Sheeps).

Helping the weak or the needy demonstrates strong characteristics. But one who freely and constantly labors without good counsel, does not produce good things. Therefore, one's foolishness is clearly demonstrated.

As a result, THE LORD who <u>already had favorable consideration for Abel's compassionate behavior</u> towards the animals he protected, accepted the presentation. But because of GOD'S preference, Cain became very angry and his DEMEANOR took a turn for the worse. So THE LORD while knowing Cain's discontentment asked, **"Why are you angry? Why are you with a bad attitude? If you DO what is RIGHT, shall you not be approved? And if you DON'T do what is right, IMMORALITY will be in store for you as well as its REQUEST. As a result, you shall have the DECISION to control it or not."** So one day while Cain and Abel were having a difference of opinions, Cain started fighting with Abel and killed him. As a result of Cain's violent act, GOD asked him, **"Where is your brother?"** He answered, "I don't know! Am I my brother's protector?" As a result of his response, GOD said to him, **"What have you done? From the ground the voice of your brother's life CALLS ME TO ACT against this INJUSTICE. For this reason, you will now be greatly TROUBLED, beginning with the land that has opened a way to take your brother's blood as a result of your Lack of Control. In addition, when you try to cultivate the land, it will NOT produce to you its strong qualities. A DESERTER AND A BAD DECISION MAKER shall you become in the world."** Because of what was about to take place, Cain said to THE LORD, "My loss is much more than I can stand. On this day, you have sent me away from the production of the land. Since this will happen, from your presence shall I be hidden; making me exactly what you said I would become. As a result, the time will come that everyone that comes to know about me, shall kill me." So because of Cain's concern of future retaliation against him, THE LORD strongly stated, **"As for ANYONE who kills Cain, seven times as much SUFFERING will be RETURNED to that individual."** As a result, <u>THE LORD established the WARNING</u> with regards to Cain's present fear. After what had been said and done, Cain left from the company of THE LORD GOD and began living in the land of **Nod** (place for DESERTERS): Its location was to the east of Eden.

<u>In spite of the effort</u> that was put to plant this cornfield, <u>it could not produce</u> something worth mentioning.

In time, while living in Nod, Cain met his mate who had his similar characteristics. As a result, when they too had their sexual intercourse experiences, they brought to the world a son whose name was **Enoch** (one who is SET APART for a particular purpose). Because of Enoch's birth, Cain built a city and named it after his son. When Enoch got older, he fathered **Irad** (one who JOINS the deserters): Irad fathered **Mehujael** (one who is DISTURBED by anxiety). Mehujael fathered **Methusael** one who BELIEVES in the worship of gods). Methusael fathered **Lamech** (one who DOES NOT practice self-control). Lamech not exercising self-control, choose for himself two women: The name of the first woman was **Adah** (one who is WORTH having). The name of the second woman was **Zillah** (one who is a CONSTANT companion). As a result of their association, Adah became pregnant and gave birth to a son named **Jabal** (one who is QUICK to act). He later became the ancestor of those who similarly LIVE in encampments and have farm animals. Now Jabal had a brother whose name was **Jubal** (one who ENJOYS music). Jubal became the ancestor of all who similarly PLAY musical instruments. In addition to Adah giving birth, Zillah also gave birth to a son named **Tubal-Cain** (one who CAUSES violence and chaos). He became the pioneer of EVERY CRAFTSMEN that specialized in Brass and Iron. Besides having Tubal-Cain, Zillah also gave birth to a daughter named **Naamah** (<u>one who is NOT violent or chaotic</u>). One day Lamech said to Adah and Zillah, "My companions, listen carefully, because I have killed a man that has the same reputation that I have. One who was still young, a sufferer like me. If Cain shall be avenged seven times as much, without a doubt I should be avenged seventy-seven times as many."

With the invention of gunpowder, <u>some society members decided</u> to become more creative in order to "better" deal with the problems of life.

Adam and Eve while living in exile, again had a son whom they named **Seth** (<u>ONE WHO IS GIVEN AS A GIFT FOR LOSS AND SUFFERING</u>). As a result, Eve said, "GOD has decided to give me another descendant to take the place of Abel, whom Cain killed." When Seth got older, he also fathered a son whom he named **Enos** (<u>ONE WHO WILL ULTIMATELY DIE ONE DAY</u>): Soon afterwards, a <u>generation of conscientious</u> HUMAN BEINGS began to ASK THE LORD for HELP.

These are the CONSCIENTIOUS GENERATIONS of Adam and Eve that have been kept for remembrance from the time that GOD formed them male and female, having ACCEPTABLE qualities. They were set apart for GOD'S special purpose and given the name (ADAM), at the same time that they were being considered.

The following well-known human beings of the past, clearly demonstrated that <u>we, too, can decide to follow the will of God</u> with peace and hope.

While many people continue to consider those who <u>prefer peaceful and hopeful means to confront the wrong of this life</u> as being unpatriotic, ignorant, unrealistic, foolish, and passive; <u>know that God has considered</u> the peaceful and hopeful fit to receive the ultimate <u>gift</u> of SALVATION.

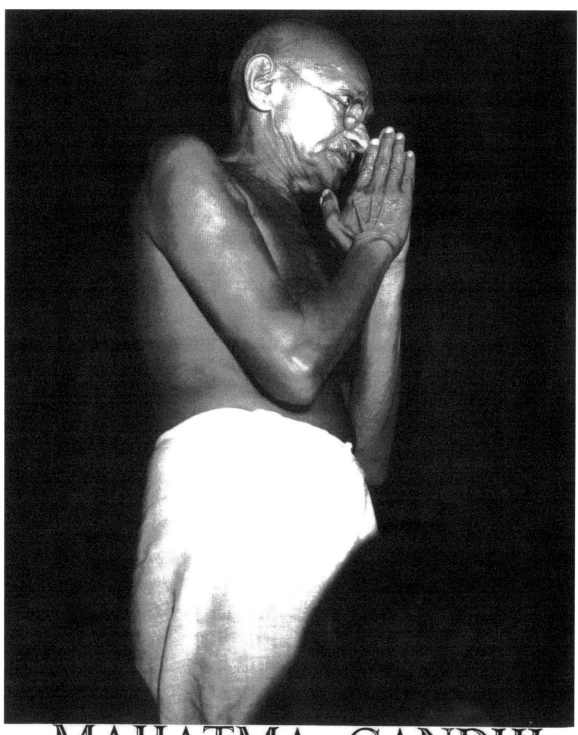

MAHATMA GANDHI
Assasinated in India 1-30-1948

When Adam was 130 years old, he fathered Seth, his third son, who had his characteristics. After the birth of Seth, Adam continued to increase the size of his descendants. The total number of years that Adam lived were 930 years. When Seth was 105 years old, he fathered **Enos.** After the birth of Enos, Seth continued to increase the size of his descendants. The total number of years that Seth lived were 912 years. When Enos was 90 years old, he fathered **Cainan** (<u>ONE WHO PRACTICES SELF-CONTROL</u>). After the birth of Cainan, Enos continued to increase the size of his descendants. The total number of years that Enos lived were 905 years. When Cainan was 70 years old, he fathered **Mahalaleel** (<u>ONE WHO DEMONSTRATES ADMIRATION FOR GOD</u>). After the birth of Mahalaleel, Cainan continued to increase the size of his descendants. The total number of years that Cainan lived were 910 years. When Mahalaleel was 65 years old, he fathered **Jared** (<u>ONE WHO WILL RECEIVE AND CONTINUE WHAT HE IS TAUGHT</u>). After the birth of Jared, Mahalaleel continued to increase the size of his descendants. The total number of years that Mahalaleel lived were 895 years. When Jared was 162 years old, he fathered **Enoch**—<u>ONE WHO IS DEVOTED TO GOD'S SPECIAL PURPOSE</u>. After the birth of Enoch, Jared continued to increase the size of his descendants. The total number of years that Jared lived were 962 years. When Enoch was 65 years old, he fathered **Methuselah** (<u>ONE WHO IS SUDDENLY CAUSED TO LEAVE</u>). Even after the birth of Methuselah, <u>Enoch followed in GOD'S way of life</u> for 300 years, <u>although</u> he continued to increase the size of his descendants. The total number of years that <u>Enoch stayed on earth</u> were <u>365 years</u>. **Enoch NEVER suffered the DISTRESSFULNESS of death** like his ancestors. <u>Instead, **GOD SAVED him from it and took him away from the difficulties of the world because of his DEDICATION**</u>—This special act of preference and love by our Creator, is the first example of salvation which God has prepared to do again for those who live or have died for His great purpose.

These valid concerns of man-kind, will not go unfulfilled! And know for certain, that REVENGE will be RIGHTLY taken.

Assassinated in Egypt 10-6-81

ANWAR el-SADAT

Assassinated in California 6-5-68

ROBERT KENNEDY

P E A C E

F R E E D O M

MALCOLM X

Assassinated in New York 2-21-65

J U S T I C E

D I G N I T Y

JOHN F.

Kennedy

Assassinated in Texas 11-22-63

Oscar Romero

Assassinated in El Salvador 3-24-80

When Methuselah was 187 years old, he fathered **Lamech** (<u>ONE WHO IS NOT EASILY INFLUENCED BY NEGATIVITY</u>). After the birth of Lamech, Methuselah continued to increase the size of his descendants. The total number of years that Methuselah lived were 969 years. When Lamech was 182 years old, he fathered a son whom he named **Noah** (<u>ONE WHO IS **NOT** AT WAR WITH GOD</u>). Because of Noah's birth, Lamech said, "<u>This child shall make our tough way of living easier</u> as a result of the land that GOD spoke against." After the birth of Noah, Lamech continued to increase the size of his descendants. The total number of years that Lamech lived were <u>777</u> years.

Medgar Evers

Assasinated in Mississippi 6-12-63

People of Today! We <u>must</u> know and remember! that the best and most effective weapon we have to combat the injustices of the world, is the WORD of GOD! because it contains the great power to <u>convict</u> as well as the great power to <u>approve</u>.

Assasinated in Tennessee 4-4-68

1-13-03

When Noah was 500 years old, he fathered three sons: **Shem** (<u>ONE WHO IS CHOSEN FOR GOD'S SPECIAL PURPOSE</u>), **Ham** (one who is IMPASSIONED) and **Japheth** (one who will become WELL-KNOWN). Because of all the existing generations, families began to increase on the surface of the earth. As a result, the birth of many female descendants began to occur. As time went by, the descendants of the conscientious followers of GOD, started to consider the daughters that were born to the unconscientous families, to be DESIRABLE. Because of this, they DECIDED to take as many of them for themselves to be their sexual companions. When this occurred, THE LORD said, **"My nature SHALL NOT ALWAYS STRUGGLE with man-kind, because they are PRONE TO MAKE MISTAKES. Now their time of being mentally and physically stable shall be 120 years."** During this period of time, there were huge beings in the world. Beings who had continued to exist even after <u>the descendants of the followers of GOD committed the UNACCEPTABLE ACTS</u> in which they also fathered children through the many women they had selected. These same descendants like in past times, became authoritative and famous figures in the world. In addition to this, <u>GOD observed that the IMMORAL BEHAVIOR OF MAN-KIND was occurring alot in the world</u>, and that <u>their ONLY BELIEF was to continue to cause HARM</u>. As a result, GOD was **DEEPLY OFFENDED** by their actions. Actions, that clearly demonstrated that they had <u>ABANDONED</u> GOD. This without a doubt, brought GOD GREAT **SADNESS**. So because of their choice of actions,GOD said, **"I will put an END to man-kind whom I have made to live on Earth; both male and female and all the animals in it, because I am DISAPPOINTED in having made them."**

The cruel acts of <u>molestation</u>, <u>abuse</u>, and <u>rape</u> on children and women, is a selfish attack on the victims' true dignity and freedom, which <u>many have taken for granted because of fame and money</u>. Therefore, those who take part in this brutality, <u>begin to expect</u> your JUST REWARD, from the ONE who has witnessed your UNGODLY behavior.

Sins of the Father

When I was raped as a teenager, I couldn't ask
our priest for help—because he was the attacker. Now, with
dozens of his other victims, I am finally getting justice.

PLAYMATE
REUNION

Las Vegas' Sexiest Topless Revue

The weapons of destruction that have <u>caused great tension and brought many lifes to a standstill</u> since their development, <u>continue to be perfected by the world's proud, ambitious and frightened intellectuals.</u> Because of this mind set, the thing that has been spoken about (World War III); will eventually come.

The different kinds of <u>hate crimes that are being committed</u> in the world by individuals with their <u>own agendas</u>, <u>will not go unpunished.</u>

The AFFLICTION of the Enslaved in the world is growing
more and more each day. Yet the oppressors continue
to Physically and Mentally chain their fellow Human
Beings for worldy gains. Therefore, their WICKED
ACTS are clearly demonstarting to GOD—THE
AVENGER OF ALL UNGODLINESS, that they
too are worthy to receive the FATE that
AWAITS the Prince of Darkness—One
who Does Not Have Our Best
Interest In Mind.

The world's <u>eagerness</u> to make life easier and meaningful, has ultimately made it possible for the Forces of Darkness—God's true enemies—to <u>manipulate the hearts and minds</u> of Human Beings. Therefore, Judgement Day must come!

The distillation process converts grains and fruits into alcohol.

inside the Internet

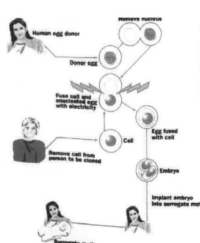

Celebrity Sheep Has Died at Age 6

Dolly, the first mammal to be cloned from adult DNA, was put down by lethal injection Feb. 14, 2003. Prior to her death, Dolly had been suffering from lung cancer and crippling arthritis. Although most Finn Dorset sheep live to be 11 to 12 years of age, postmortem examination of Dolly seemed to indicate that, other than her cancer and arthritis, she appeared to be quite normal. The unnamed sheep from which Dolly was cloned had died several years prior to her creation. Dolly was a mother to six lambs, bred the old-fashioned way.

These are <u>few of the many manipulating substances</u>, which many seek for <u>self</u> gratification and riches. But they <u>will not at all</u> serve as an excuse, when the <u>great day</u> of the LORD comes.

On the other hand, Noah received GOD'S APPROVAL.

1-21-03

These are the characteristics that set Noah apart from those whom GOD DISAPPROVED OF: He demostrated the ability to UNDERSTAND the concept of right and wrong. He was NOT INVOLVED with the negative things that were happening around him. As a result of his conscientious behavior, <u>Noah kept himself CONNECTED WITH GOD</u>. By this time, Noah had already fathered three sons. A time when the world was being occupied by continuous acts of **VIOLENCE** and many other **IMMORALITIES**. As for GOD, after OBSERVING the condition that the world was in, decided to INFORM as well as GUIDE Noah, about what was soon to take place and what he should PREPARE to do in order to be PROTECTED.

1-25-03

These are the special instructions that GOD gave to Noah: **1. To construct a chest** (object used to store valuables) **with gopher wood** (such wood no longer exist). **2. To make rooms inside of it. 3. To cover the seams of the chest inside and out with tar** (a thick, black, sticky substance obtained by the distillation of wood or coal). GOD also gave Noah detailed instructions about the dimensions that the chest and everything in it should be. After the completion of the chest, GOD proceeded to say to Noah **"With you will I SET MY FIRM AND LASTING UNION. Because of this, you shall ENTER the chest along with your mate, sons and their particular partner. In addition, choose a pair of all kinds of animals that are male and female to go into the chest, so they can be kept alive with you. Also gather for yourselves all types of foods, because they will serve as nourishment for you all."** So Noah did everything that was INSTRUCTED to him by GOD. As a result of Noah's OBEDIENCE, GOD continued to DIRECT him by saying, **"Go into the chest, you and all your household, because in you have I observed CONSCIOUS BEHAVIOR during these times."** GOD then BEGAN to give Noah specific instructions about the type of animals that would continue to reproduce on earth. In addition to this, GOD said, **"In HONOR of the SEVENTH DAY, I will bring about a DEVASTATING storm to be on earth for 40 days and 40 nights in order to DO AWAY with EVERY LIVING THING that I have made."** Noah, again did everything as he had been instructed.

34

Noah was 600 years old when all the world became covered by the great outpouring of rain, which included the flowing and rising waters that sprayed up from beneath the huge Oceans of the Earth. While this was occurring, everyone inside the large chest had a sense of security as it was being raised over the highest of landforms: <u>Plains</u>, <u>Plateaus</u>, <u>Hills</u>, and <u>Mountains</u>. As a result, the waters did what they were COMMANDED to do against ALL the earth's creations. When all was said and done, **EVERY HUMAN BEING, EVERY ANIMAL, and EVERY MATERIAL** that existed, DIED. The waters from <u>ABOVE</u> the earth, <u>AROUND</u> the earth, and <u>BENEATH</u> the earth had been victorious throughout the world. A victory that continued for 150 days. During this period of time, GOD kept the survivors in mind as they lived aboard the chest. As a result, the rising waters that GOD had caused to explode from the bottom of the great oceans, along with the excess water that fell from the sky, were made to stop. The rain was kept to a limit as the floodwaters began to frequently leave the earth. After the COMPLETE DESTRUCTION of those that GOD greatly disapproved of, the waters at the end of five months were reduced.

Thunder clouds.

Beginning of rain.

Snow Storm.

Tornado and lightning.

Ocean begins to calm down.

Eruption from the ocean floor.

1-30-03

Two months after the reduction of floodwaters began to occur, the treasure chest became motionless atop the mountains of **Ararat** (place of high ground). By the tenth month, as the waters continued to decrease, the remaining mountaintops of the earth began to appear. At the conclusion of the ANNIHILATION, Noah opened the single window of the chest, and drove out a large bird in order for it to find dry land. Besides the large bird that Noah repeatedly sent out, he also sent a diving bird into the water in order to know the deepness that the waters were from the ground of the earth. But in the bird's labor to find ground level, it could not reach the bottom. As a result, it would swim back to Noah.

2-9-03

After waiting a few days, Noah again sent the diving bird. But this time, it returned to Noah with an olive leaf on its beak.

As a result, Noah now knew that the waters were reducing and that new life forms were beginning to grow. After having this important information, Noah again waited a few more days (7), before deciding to send the large bird on the same mission of finding dry land. On that day the bird found pasture and it did not return to Noah. So on Noah's 601 year of living, the large quantities of water had soaked through the lands. After realizing that there was dry land, Noah and his family began to remove the roof from the chest.

GOD again spoke to Noah saying, **"You and all that are with you, come out the TREASURE chest so that you may REPRODUCE greatly and abundantly on earth."** As a result, they all came out in pairs with the same understanding. As the different types of animals began to reproduce themselves, Noah carefully chose a few of them (<u>animals that had no defects</u>) and built a mound in order to prepare them for THE LORD as a burnt gift. As a result of this CAREFUL expression of gratitude, THE LORD passionately said, **"Because of man-kinds <u>PREDICAMENT</u> of wanting to be GOOD, HEALTHY, HAPPY, COMFORTABLE, AND PROSPEROUS, I will NOT bring destruction to the earth, NOR will I do away with ALL living things again, as I have done. Because from the beginning of their development** (referring to Adam and Eve's time in the Garden), **they have had the capabilities to MAKE DECISIONS. So while the world continues to exist: <u>The Planting of Seeds</u>, <u>The Gathering of Crops</u>, <u>The Weather</u>, <u>The Seasons</u>, and <u>The 24 hours of Each Day</u>, shall NOT be put to an END."** After this strong declaration, GOD revealed to Noah and his companions the HOPE for their future, by telling them: <u>To be productive</u> in the things they do on earth; <u>To increase</u> their numbers on earth; and <u>To care</u> for the things that are on the earth.

The <u>sacrificial acts</u> by man-kind <u>continue to occur</u> in the world. A clear example of this, is by the <u>many lifes that are gone</u> because of Warfare; DOMESTIC and FOREIGN.

2-19-03

Once again, GOD had DECIDED to express the SAME HOPE that was DECLARED to Noah's ancestors 'Adam and Eve', BEFORE BEING PERSUADED TO IGNORE GOD'S SPECIFIC WARNING in the Garden of Eden. In addition to this, GOD said, **"The feeling of great UNEASINESS shall be on every animal of the earth. Because of this, towards your CAPABILITIES are they given over. Every animal like every plant life shall serve as NOURISHMENT for you. But meat containing the SOURCE of life, which is the BLOOD from it, you shall NOT eat. I will without a doubt CLAIM the blood of everyone's life: THROUGH THE ACTIONS OF EVERY FOUR-FOOTED ANIMAL, EVERY PERSON, AND EVERY PERSON'S RELATIVE, WILL I CLAIM THAT LIFE.** Any person that puts another person's life to an end, through the actions of another shall that life be taken, because PEOPLE were made having GODLY CHARACTERISTICS—REFERRING TO THE PURSUIT OF JUSTICE. Because of these reasons, become productive and many in the world. Now I prepare my AGREEMENT with all of you and all of your FUTURE DESCENDANTS: <u>All life</u> shall NOT suddenly be stopped by floodwaters; NEITHER shall there be a flood of great <u>Size</u>, <u>Strength</u>, and <u>Height</u> to make the earth USELESS. This is the SIGN of the agreement that I make with each and every one of you IN CONSIDERATION of your CONTINUOUS DESCENT: I will put my RAINBOW in the sky <u>as a symbol</u> of the agreement between me and the world. In addition, I will CAUSE the rainbow to be seen from above the lands of the EARTH.

It is <u>FOOLISH to PERVERT</u> the meaning of **GOD'S** great symbol!

2-19-03

Because of this, I will KEEP IN MIND THE EVERLASTING AGREEMENT that I have put in place between ME-AND-YOU WHO WILL INHABIT THE EARTH."

We are all GOD'S children! But JUSTLY ENOUGH, only those who are OBEDIENT to the CALL, will be GRACIOUSLY REWARDED!!!

WHY WE CAN ONLY TRACE OUR
GENEALOGY AND HERITAGE TO A
CERTAIN POINT IN LIFE?

Motivated by <u>pride</u>, <u>ambition</u>, and <u>greed</u>, these empires like the many others that developed and ended throughout history, became strong by controlling the waterways, land, the land's mineral resources, and ultimately the people. As a result of the conquests, <u>obvious mixing of races</u>, <u>cultures</u>, and <u>sometimes renouncement of traditions</u> occurred. So as things continued to take place, our ancestors became more CONCERNED about surviving the difficult times rather than keeping up with their family tree and their belief-system. Because of these important reasons, **<u>a careful decision about</u>** WHO and WHAT, we will put our **FAITH** and **TRUST** on <u>must</u> take place.

ACCEPTING THE CIRCUMSTANCES OF THE PAST,
CAN ONLY HELP YOU GET A BETTER UNDERSTANDING
ABOUT WHAT DECISION YOU SHOULD MAKE ABOUT
YOUR FUTURE!!

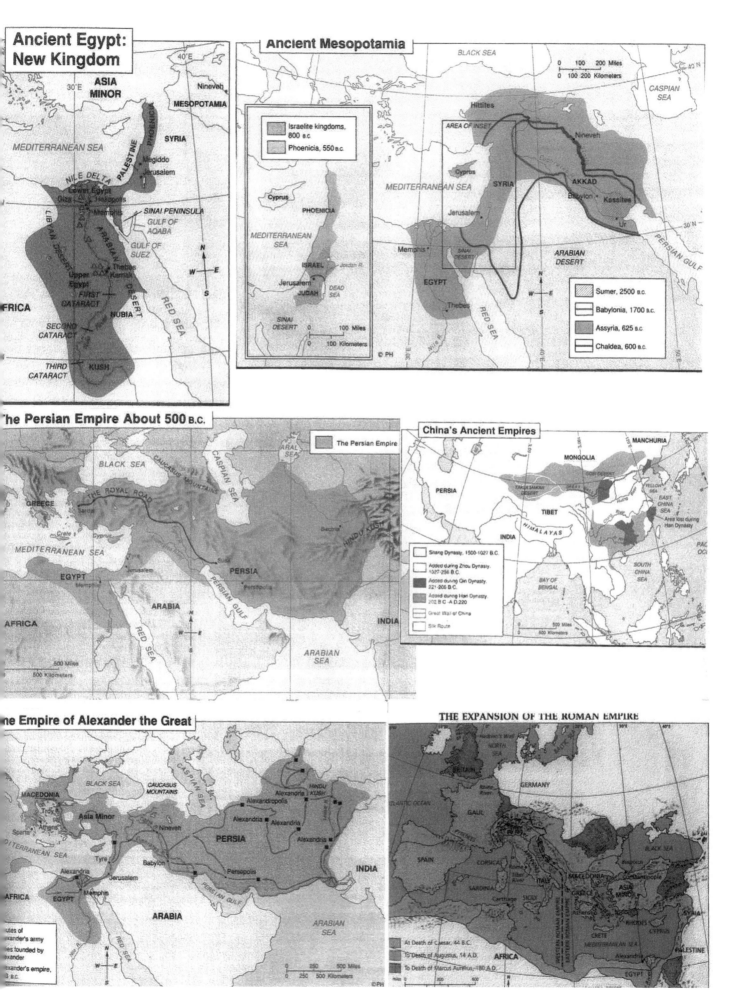

48

Principles of Communication?

ARGUE: Implies the citing of reasons or evidence to support or refute an assertion, belief, proposition, etc.

DEBATE: Implies a formal argument, usually on public questions, in contests between opposing groups.

DISCUSS: Implies a talking about something in a deliberative fashion, with varying opinions offered constructively and usually peaceful, so as to settle an issue, decide on a course of action, etc.

DISPUTE: Implies argument in which there is a clash of opposing opinions, often presented in an angry or heated manner.

Source: Webster s New World Dictionary Third College Edition

Principles of Being Convinced?

AGNOSTIC: One who questions the existence of God, heaven, etc.

ATHEIST: One who rejects all religious belief and denies the existence of God.

BELIEVER: One who mentally accepts something to be true even though absolute certainty may not be there.

DEIST: One who believes that God is a creative moving force but rejects formal religion including its doctrines of revelation, divinity, authority, etc.

FREE-THINKER: One who rejects a principle, doctrine, or belief held to be true by any particular group or groups.

INFIDEL: One who does not believe in a certain religion or one that is more dominant than others.

UNBELIEVER: One who does not accept any religious belief.

BRANCHES OF SCIENCE: Those who concern themselves with how things work after establishing and systematizing facts, principles, and methods through experiments and possible explainations.

HISTORIANS: Those who concern themselves with history. As a result, they write about it.

RELIGIOUS SECTS: Any group of people having a common leadership, set of opinions, philosophical doctrines, political principles, ect.

Source:Webster s New World Dictionary Third College Edition

GOD'S Principles of Being Convinced!

FAITH: Is complete ACCEPTANCE of <u>GOD</u> even in the absence of proof and especially of things not supported by reason.

TRUST: Is the ASSURANCE by the direct knowledge of the <u>MESSIAH</u> —one who has been set apart to be deeply RESPECTED and LOVED. This principle can occur without the conscious use of reasoning.

Source: King James Holy Bible

NAHUM

THE LORD is slow to anger and great in power, and WILL NOT AT ALL ACQUIT the wicked: THE LORD has his WAY IN DEALING with evilness and its attack. As a result, its effect is UNDER COMPLETE CONTROL. 1:3

THE LORD is good, a strong hold IN THE TIME OF TROUBLE; and HE KNOWS them that TRUST IN HIM. 1:7

LUKE

When YOU pray, say: Our FATHER, Who Is In Heaven, HIGHLY IMPORTANT IS YOUR NAME; Your Kingdom Come, Your Will Be Done, On Earth, As It Is In Heaven; Give Us Each Day, Our Daily Lives, FORGIVE Us Our Bad Acts, Because We Also FORGIVE Everyone That Does Wrong Against Us; GUIDE Us Away From The Persuasion Of Immorality, But SAVE Us From It. 11:24

GIFTS

Having been in the darkness of understanding, I give you to UNDERSTAND, that NO HUMAN BEING, SPEAKING THROUGH THE **CHARACTER** of **GOD,** mentions **JESUS**—one who saves—as having an EVIL FATE. In addition, NO HUMAN BEING can say, that JESUS is THE **LORD,** but THROUGH THE **Set Apart and Honorable Character of GOD:** Now there are VARIETIES of Gifts, but THE **SAME** CHARACTER. As a result, there are DIFFERENCES of ADMINISTRATION, but THE **SAME** LORD. In addition, there are VARIETIES of OPERATIONS, but it is the **SAME** GOD that WORKS **ALL** in **ALL.** But THE EVIDENCE of THE CHARACTER is GIVEN to **EVERY** HUMAN BEING to BENEFIT from **IT ALL.**

Because to one is given through THE CHARACTERISTICS OF GOD the word of **Wisdom;** to another the word of **Knowledge** through the same CHARACTER; to another **Faith** through the same CHARACTER; to another the gifts of **Healing** through the same CHARACTER; to another the working of **Miracles;** to another **Prophecy;** to another **Discerning of Characteristics;** to another **Different Kinds of Languages;** to another the **Interpretation of Languages.**

But **All** these works are ONE and the SAME CHARACTER, divided to EVERY HUMAN BEING INDIVIDUALLY as **GOD** DECIDES.

1 CORINTHIANS 12

Verses 3-11

2-8-03

THE WORD OF GOD SPEAKS WITH URGENCY AND CLARITY:

TO THE HEARTS OF THOSE WHO ARE WILLING TO KNOW AND LISTEN ATTENTIVELY, BECAUSE <u>THE **WORD**</u> CONTAINS THE **PROMISE** THAT IS **ALREADY** IN PLACE FOR THOSE WHO <u>ACCEPT</u> OR <u>DENY</u> THE **EVERLASTING ONE WHO SAVES.**

3-14-03

A MESSAGE TO THOSE WHO CONSISTENTLY QUESTION THE VALIDITY OF GOD'S PURPOSEFUL WORD:

EACH DAY YOU LIVE IS AN **OPPORTUNITY** TO DECIDE AND PREPARE, SO STOP YOUR STUBBORNESS BECAUSE TOMORROW MIGHT NOT COME AS YOU EXPECT.

3-24-03

A MESSAGE TO THE CLERGY OF THE WORLD WHO TRULY DESIRE
TO HAVE THE APPROVAL OF THE TRUE AND ONLY GOD:
DO NOT ALLOW YOUR ESTABLISHMENT TO BECOME
UNRELIABLE TO THE HOPEFUL.

In1994, approximately 800,000 Tutsi—children, women, and men—of Africa, were <u>Massacred</u> as a result of RESENTMENT that turned into RAGE. But the MOST <u>disappointing</u> and <u>disturbing</u> thing that occurred during that time was that those who could have helped against the <u>MERCILESS</u> killing; CHOSE NOT TO.

6-11-03

A MESSAGE TO ALL WHO ARE WILLING TO SURRENDER
THEIR HEARTS—THE PART THAT FEELS, DESIRES, HATES,
AND LOVES—TO GOD:

IN YOUR **SURRENDER**, YOU WILL RECEIVE THE UNDERSTANDING
OF THE **TRUST** THAT LEADS TO **PEACE EVERLASTING.**

* Lamentations of JEREMIAH 3:26
It is good that PEOPLE of the world should both HOPE and
PEACEFULLY WAIT for **THE SALVATION OF THE LORD.**

*JOHN 3:16
BECAUSE **GOD** LOVED MAN-KIND SO MUCH, **GOD** GAVE THE ONLY
PRODUCED **SON;** THAT WHOEVER HAS TRUST IN **HIM,** SHOULD NOT
CONTINUE IN A STATE OF SUFFERING, BUT HAVE EVERLASTING LIFE.

"IGNORANCE
IS NO EXCUSE,"
IT'S A CHOICE!

CHOOSE THIS DAY TO REPRESENT
THE ONE AND ONLY SAVIOR!

JAH LOVE

STUDY TO PRESENT YOUR-
SELF SATISFACTORY TO GOD:
A PERSON THAT DOES THE
WORK OF GOD WITHOUT
SHAME AND WHO PROPERLY
RECOGNIZES THE WORD OF
TRUTH.

2 Timothy 2:15

Printed in the United States
By Bookmasters